BONSAI

Supervised by Kyuzo Murata

# INTRODUCTORY
# BONSAI
## and the care and use of
## bonsai tools
by
MASAKUNI KAWASUMI

**JAPAN PUBLICATIONS, INC.**

*Tokyo & San Francisco*

**Inclined juniper group.**
In the possession of Mrs. Patricia Nixon.
(Presented by Ben T. Suzuki)

# Preface

In recent years, English-language books on bonsai, ranging from beginners' manuals to works for the near professional, have appeared in large numbers; but in this book I intend to discuss from the purely practical bonsai standpoint the correct selection and use of bonsai tools and certain problem points that the bonsai cultivator will encounter. For example, one of the first difficulties involves soils. There are a number of special Japanese soils used in bonsai cultivation. But the plants in America, Europe, Australia, and other parts of the world are accustomed to their own soils; one cannot always expect good results from suddenly forcing bonsai versions of these plants to live in soils imported from Japan. The finest soil for bonsai is one that retains water, but that also drains well and that allows free passage of air. Whether the soil should be acid, neutral, or alkali may be judged from the nature of the soil in which the plant intended for bonsai training grows naturally. In short, if the soil the plant lives in meets the three requirements I mentioned, it is the best one to use.

Unfortunately, however, the situation is not always as simple as this. In almost all cases, bonsai plants are kept in areas far removed—consequently, different in climate and soil conditions—from their natural habitat. Under such conditions, the soil of the natural habitat is sometimes suitable, but often an entirely different soil is preferable. Furthermore, even in cases in which the soil of the natural habitat is suitable for bonsai purposes, it is not always readily available. One is then well advised to use a soil that resembles that of the plant's natural habitat, but one need not always limit one's choices entirely to soils of this kind. For instance, in Japan trees of the pine family spring up naturally along the seashore and in mountainous regions. In the Kansai area, the district in which Osaka and Kyoto are located, pure river sand is used almost exclusively in pine bonsai. In the Kanto Plains, on the other hand, red soil with a mixture of Kiryu-sand is used. The choices depend

When my father departed his home fifty five years ago, planted many young Japanese cypress on the hill of his villege, shrine, and those plants grow very fine now. So I want to show those fine style.

*Namban-giseru;* height 8 inches. The Emperor of Japan raises bonsai of this kind at the palace in Tokyo. This one is combined with Japanese pampas grass.

Gingko 50 years old; height 26 inches.

Maple (*kaede*) group planting 25 years old; height 18.5 inches. This style is often called a thousand-tree group planting.

Maple with stone 30 years old; height 15 inches.

# 1. Grafts

Grafting is a method whereby a branch, bud, or root cut from a living plant is attached to another plant of either the same or a very close species in such a way as to produce a new plant. The plant to which the graft is made is called the parent stock, and the grafted part is called the graft. One of the outstanding points about grafting is that the graft, possessing exactly the same hereditary characteristic as the plant from which it is cut, blooms or bears fruit much faster than plants raised from nature or from cuttings. Aside from the somewhat special cases of the *nishiki* pine and the five-needle (*goyo*) pine, grafting is most generally used in growing flowering or fruit-bearing plants.

## Various Methods

1. Branch grafting. Examples: *nishiki* pine (black pines or small red pines), five-needle pine (black pines or small red pines), plum (fruit-bearing plums), cherries (fruit-bearing cherries, or cuttings of wild mountain cherries), Japanese magnolias (*kobushi*), roses (wild roses), loquat (fruit-bearing loquat), pears (wild pears), or persimmons (miniature persimmons).

Note: the plants in parentheses are well suited to this method.

2. Bud grafting. Examples: peaches, pears, or roses.
3. Base grafting. Examples: plums, quince, or ginkgo.
4. Top grafting.

Although each of these grafting methods has its special characteristics, branch grafting is the most frequently used in bonsai. Root grafting is next most widely used.

## Proper Seasons for Grafting

The best time for branch grafting is spring, before the new buds appear. Results are poor if grafts are either too early or too late. For root grafts, the best time is about October. Buds are best grafted after the spring rains and until about early September.

### Preparing the Parent Stock

Select a parent that is strong, well rooted, and young for the sake of easy grafting.

*Branches*

In grafting branches for *nishiki* pines, five-needle pines, black pines, and red pines, select a sapling two years old. It may be wild stock, a garden plant, or another potted plant.

For flowering or fruit-bearing trees select either a sapling that is two or three years old or cut a newly developed branch from as low a position on a parent tree. Always select young branches for grafts since they respond much better to the process. The reasons for selecting a newly developed branch from a low position on an old parent tree is this: the grafting process renews the branch and enables the cultivator to produce a small, compact bonsai.

*Roots*

Root grafts are generally used to rejuvenate old, tired bonsai or to improve root spread. Therefore, from a plant of either the same or a very closely related species, select healthy, young roots that have put out many fine rootlets and root hairs. Since the new root will be grafted at the place where the trunk of the bonsai enters the ground, it might be thought of as the stock. Its relationship to the plant, then, is the direct opposite of that of a branch graft.

### Selecting a Graft

The graft (also called the scion) will become either the trunk or a branch of the bonsai and is consequently very important. For that reason it must be taken from a healthy plant. The graft branch must be one that came out in the spring of the year preceding the one in which it will be cut. It must be sturdy and about half developed. After cutting, thrust it, cut end first, into wet sand and put it in a place where wind does not reach it.

## Tools Needed for Grafting

**a**   A small, sharp grafting knife.

**b**   Pruning scissors for cutting the stock and for trimming away excess roots.

**c**   Plastic tape (without adhesive).

**d**   An adhesive paste.

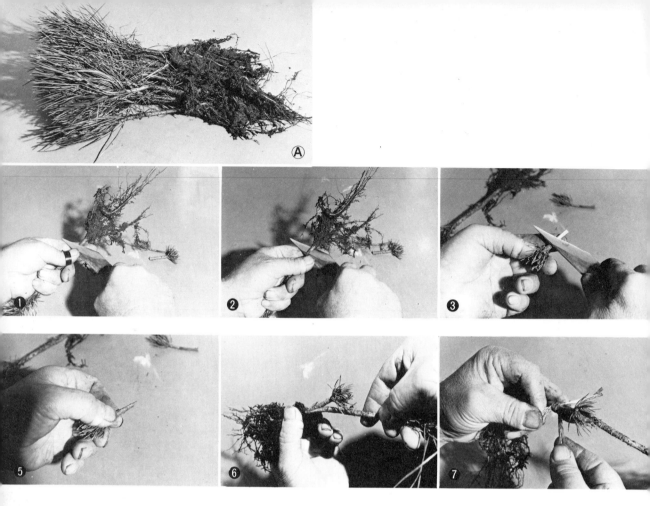

## Grafting Techniques

1.   *Root Grafting ( five-needle pine)*
*The stock*—two-year-old black pine (photograph Ⓐ).
*Grafts*—branches of five-needle pine that first came out in the spring of the preceding year (photograph Ⓑ).

❶   First make a cut. (Note: carefully observe the ways in which the stock and the grafting knife are held).

❷   The angle of the cut is about five degrees. The knife enters the woody part of the base of the stem and proceeds to the base. It cuts through about one-third of the thickness of the trunk.

❸   Trimming the graft. The first cut is at about fifty degrees.

❹   The second cut is made on the opposite side of the graft; it should be slightly long and should form an angle of about forty-five degrees with the first cut.

❺   The properly trimmed graft.

❻ Inserting the graft into the stock. The growth layers of the graft and the stock must coincide with each other and must be held tightly together. Even when the thickness of the two are different so that both do not match, at least one must beheld very firmly in place.

❼ Winding the tape. Instead of tying, it is possible to fix the tape in-place with an adhesive.

❽ The stock and the new graft.

❾ Potting the stock. Use an unglazed pot. Two important points to remember when potting are these. The roots of the stock must be well spread through the entire pot to prevent the development of strange and often very troublesome twists. Be certain that the soil reaches the point of graft.

❿ Enlargement of the graft. Water the plant well, but do not directly wet the grafted place.

⓫ Comparison of growth. The graft on the right has been growing on the stock for a year. The branch part of the stock has been cut off at the soil line.

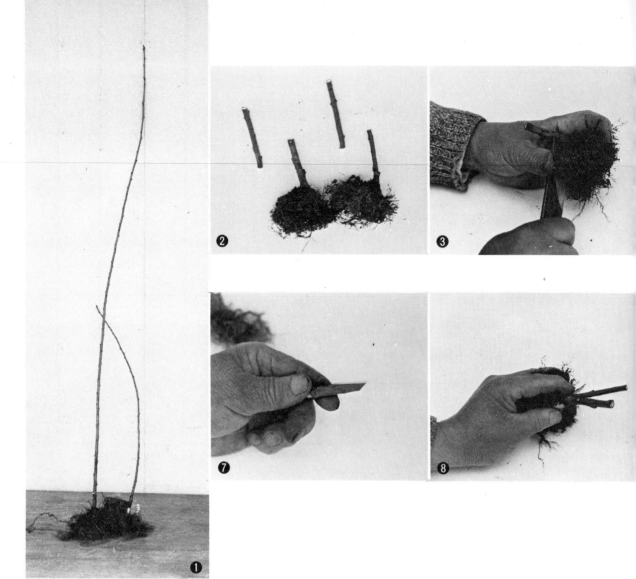

## 2. Base Grafting (plum)

**①** Plum stock.

Always use a cutting from wild plum as stock.

**②** Cut the stock to a length of about two inches. Cut the graft to about the same length.

**③** Make an incision running to the base of the stock as shown in the photograph. The cut should be at about a five-degree angle, and at the base it should extend across about one-third of the circumference of the trunk. Pay special attention to the ways in which one must hold the knife and the stock.

**④** Next trim the graft.

**⑤** The first cut is made at about a fifty-degree angle.

**⑥** Next trim the opposite side. This cut must be somewhat long.

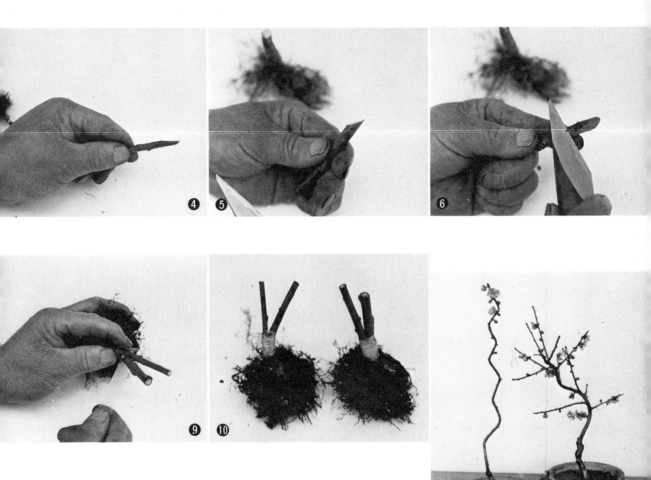

⓻ The second cut must form about a forty-five-degree angle with the first.

⓼ Insert the graft into the stock, taking care to align the growth layers.

⓽ Securely wrap the base of the stock and the graft with plastic tape. Fix it in place with glue.

⓾ Two examples of completed grafts.

⓫ The graft on the left is one year old; that in the middle is two years old (small wild plum); that on the right is two years old (literati-style tree).

⓬ Enlargement of a base graft that is one year old.

⓭ Enlargement of a base graft that is two years old.

3. *Top Grafting.* (*Japanese holly*)
❶ Stock (Japanese holly).
❷ Stock and grafts.
❸ The first cut, at the end of the stock, is to smooth the cut surface.
❹ Make a vertical cut running at the edge of and parallel with the woody part of the trunk (see the following illus.). The graft is trimmed as for the plum.
❺ Inserting the graft into the stock.
❻ The growth layers of the two must align when the graft has been fully inserted.
❼ Wrap with tape.
❽ Three times around the stock and graft should be sufficient.
❾ Fix the tape in place with an adhesive.
❿ Completed grafts. When grafts are numerous, instead of potting them, plant them in a field.

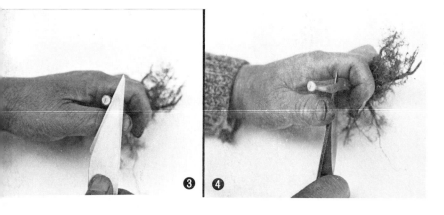

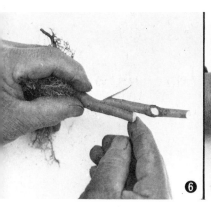

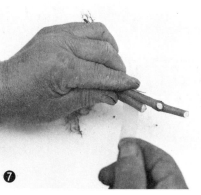

The Growth Layers

The woody Part
of The Trunk

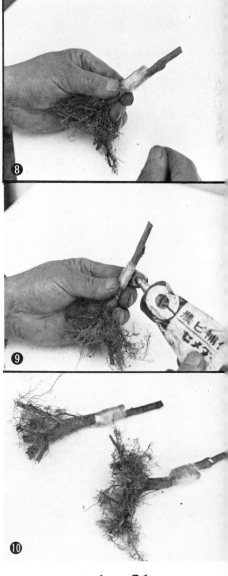

⓫　Exactly one year after grafting.

⓬　Englargement of the graft.

⓭　Exactly two years after the graft.

⓮　Enlargement of the graft.

⓯　A ten-year-old graft.

⓰　Enlargement of the graft.

### 4. *Grafting of Deciduous Trees*

Suitable seasons and grafting methods are identical to those for the pines.

❶ Branch graft (apple)
Hime-kokko. The graft was made one year before this photograph was taken.

❷ This tree stayed in a field one year after the graft was made.

❸ One year after a top graft on a weeping plum.

❹ Small wild plums. The graft on the left was made two years before and that on the right seven years before the photograph was taken.

❺ Enlargement of a top graft on a weeping plum.

With the recent development of waterproof plastic tapes it has become easy to prevent water from entering the graft cuts. Consequently, good grafts can be made with relative ease if one observes these rules. Use a sharp knife to cut the craft and stock and make sure the angles of the cuts are correct. When inserting the graft be sure to align its growth layer with that of the stock. After grafting and planting, keep the plants in a place where about half the day they are in shade and where the wind does not blow on them. For about three weeks water them sufficiently that they never dry out. When making only a small number of grafts, plant them in pots; but when the grafted plants are numerous, plant them in an open field.

**❶ Grafted plants in an open field.**

(from the front) Five-needle pine, Chinese quince, apple, weeping plum. All of them were grafted two months before the photograph was made.

**❷ *Nishiki* pine.**

**❸ Chinese quince.**

**❹ Apple (*Hime-Kokko*).**

**❺ Cherry (*Asahiyama*).**

**❻ Five-needle pine.**

In the foreground is Akahane hawthorne.

**❼ Weeping plum**

All of these were grafted two months before the photographs were taken.

❽ Grafted Japanese holly, four months after the grafts were made. There are berries on all the perfectly grafted specimens. This large specimen has a circumference at the roots of about fifteen inches. ❾ Enlargement of the graft.

**24** GRAFTS

# 2. Obtaining Wild Materials

Grafting is one way of reproducing plants, but it also possible to go to the mountains and forests to obtain suitable wild materials. In addition, it is possible to use cuttings from trees, to separate plant groups into individual plants, and to perform a process known as layering. Finally it is possible to raise many plants from seeds. In this section, I shall explain the first of these methods: obtaining wild materials.

*Bonsai from Wild Materials*

Anyone who goes on a picnic, hiking, or just for a walk is bound to see countless trees, grasses, and other plants thriving in their natural conditions. Some of them are ornamented with beautiful flowers; some are borne down under the weight of branches laden with fruit. Sometimes one sees a wonderful towering evergreen bent, but still proud, under its hundred years of age and with the scars from wounds it has sustained in the battle to remain alive in the changing seasonal conditions of the natural world. As they have thrilled to the beauty of nature, many people have probably longed to dig up a few plants and take them home as remembrances of the beauty they had enjoyed.

But only after they have been provided with the good natural soil and the blessings of heaven to which they have grown accustomed will these plants live. No matter how carefully one digs them up, wraps them, and plants them upon returning to one's home, many of them die. Of course, not all, but a large percentage. Some grasses, with their wide root masses, live and bloom and bear fruit or berries. Trees that one may bring home, should be fairly old, thick trunked, and well formed. One may simply plant them as they are. If they live, they provide a handsome sight. There is no easier or faster way to obtain material for bonsai than this. Indeed, many of the most famous of all bonsai of a wide variety of kinds have been developed from formerly untouched trees brought from the mountains and fields.

### Suitable Seasons for Transplanting

This of course varies to an extent with the location, climate, kind of plant, and with the skill of the person doing the digging. In general, however, the best time for most plants and trees to be transplanted from a wild habitat is in the spring immediately after the buds have begun to appear and before the roots are active. At this time, the output of new roots is small, the roots themselves are inactive, and therefore damage in transplanting is small while chances of success are great. One must be careful to realize, however, that the roots of some plants become active a month or so before the buds begin to appear. Some of the deciduous trees—notably the zelkova and the maple—are best moved during their dormant phase between fall and spring. The pines, by and large, may be moved at their most active peak in summer without suffering harm.

### Methods

1  First of all clear away all grasses and shrubs from the base of the tree. Examine the tree well from bottom to top, and cut off any low branches.

2  Dig a trench all the way around the tree. It must have a circumference about five or six times the circumference of the trunk of the tree.

3  Cut all roots exposed in the trench. Use root-cutters for thick roots.

4  Dig out as shown in the chart.

5  If you intend to take the tree home with the soil attached to the roots, take up as much soil as you can. Wrap it well in wet sphagnum moss and then in a sheet of plastic. If you intend to remove the soil, do so gently and wrap all of the roots well in wet sphagnum moss. Once again, wrap them in a sheet of plastic. Be especially gentle with small roots.

6  After having arrived home with the plant, cut the main root with root cutting scissors. The cut must be straight across the root. This is done to stimulate growth of smaller roots; therefore, it is an absolutely essential operation. If the plant has too many roots to fit into the pot, cut them off but trim away a proportionate amount of branches. In this instance, a slightly large pot is better; but it must not be too deep, for excess depth prevents the roots from warming and thus slows down their generative powers.

Leave the plant in this slightly large pot until the next suitable repotting season. This will allow it to build up its strength. Then when it is in good condition, it may be transplanted to a pot that blends with its size and nature. Initial potting and repotting involve the same procedures.

**7** It is also possible first to trim away the damaged roots from a wild plant that you have brought home then to prune the branches, and after doing this to plant it in the ground. In two or three years, the plant may be potted when the proper replanting season comes around.

**8** If you want to be completely sure of success, make the trench around the base of the plant as described. Cut the roots, then fill the trench in again. After one year passes, return to the spot, dig up the plant, and take it to your home for bonsai preparation. This is the safest of all methods, because small rootlets have already developed in abundance before you dig the plant up.

**9** If it is unavoidable to dig up a wild plant in a season other than the proper one for transplanting, it is essential to cut off all of the leaves, because in moving the plant one inevitably damages the roots. This reduces the plant's ability to take in moisture. Since leaves give off moisture into the air, in order to allow the plant to maintain a moisture balance, the leaves must be cut away. This is also the reason for keeping newly potted wild plants in a semi-shaded place and for watering them often with a fine spray.

**10** Never fertilize a newly potted bonsai plant until it has taken firm root (about one month after potting).

**11** Remove all of the large particles from the soil you are using for potting in order to ensure good drainage. This rule must always be observed.

**12** In summary, then, for bonsai always select a wild plant that has sufficient value to justify the labor. The roots must be well spread, the tree must stand well, and it must have at least one interesting limb. Beyond this, training and care can do something to improve a plant, but these three points must be observed or the cultivator's task is hopeless.

## Tools Needed for Taking Plants from Their Natural Habitat

   **a**  Spatula for cutting roots and a shovel.
   **b**  Large and small cutters for roots, saw, and scythe for cutting grass.
   **c**  Pruning shears No. 1 (see p. 76).
   **d**  Plastic sheet.
   **e**  Cord.
   **f**  Sphagnum moss.

# *3. Potting*

Plants that have been kept in the garden or in an open field and that have more or less completely formed and have a dense mass of small roots near the base of the trunk are ready for potting. Using a series of photographs, I shall now explain how this is done.

❶ First dig the plant up with a shovel.

❷ The mass of soil and roots should be about the size shown.

❸ This is a kind of azalea about thirty-five years old. At the base, the trunk has a diameter of about four inches. At the time of this photograph it had been cultivated in an open field for twenty years.

❹ Trim away unwanted branches where they join the trunk. Use azalea pruning shears.

**❺** Take care that the cut is in the same plane with the surface of the trunk.

**❻** Wire the good branches into the desired positions (see p. 65).

**❼** The plant after all unwanted branches have been pruned away.

**❽** Rake the surface of the soil with a hand rake.

**❾** Carefully rake the soil from the underside of the roots but be especially cautious not to injure the central section.

**❿** In the case of azaleas *all* of the soil remaining from the earlier field planting place must be removed from the roots. If it is not, even one grain of this soil could become the cause of rotting in the roots. As shown in this picture, while running water over the roots, carefully remove this soil with bamboo chopsticks.

**⓫** Use the force of the stream of water and a probe like the one shown to remove the particles of soil in places into which the bamboo chopsticks will not go.

**⓬** Be careful to remove all soil from the underside as well.

⑬ Use very sharp pruning shears to trim roots that are too long. Dull shears can cause the roots to adhere or to grow again.

⑭ In this case I am using Kanuma soil with an admixture of mountain moss; but if this is unavailable, use the soil you have on hand. In short, if the soil retains water but also drains well, it is adequate. You may think of the the moss as a kind of dam to hold in some of the moisture. In order to ensure that there will be plenty of soil under the central part of the roots, mound it in the middle of the container.

⑮ Positioning the plant. Sliding the plant on a horizontal plane to right and left to find the best position, press downward to make sure soil is rotated under the roots.

⑯ The plant has been positioned.

⑰ The wires that you will have run through the holes in the bottom of the pot in an earlier process (see p. 28) are used to fix the tree in place. Protect the roots from damage by placing small bits of rubber on top of them where they come into contact with the wire. Use pincers to position the wire.

⑱ Putting the remaining soil into the container.

⑲    Working gently to avoid damaging the roots, thrust soil among them with bamboo chopsticks.

⑳    Sweep away excess soil with a hand broom.

㉑    Cover the top of the soil with moss or sphagnum moss to prevent drying.

㉒    Water well and clean away all unsightly soil from the pot; potting is now complete.


**Tools Needed for Potting** (see pp. 76-79).

  **a**   Shovel.
  **b**   Turntable.
  **c**   Azalea pruning shears.
  **d**   Hand rake.
  **e**   Bamboo (or plastic or resin) chopsticks.
  **f**   Probe for inserting soil in tight places.
  **g**   Wire cutters, wire, and a few lengths of copper wire.
  **h**   Pincers.
  **i**   Pruning shears.

# 4. Bonsai with Stones

These striking compositions enable one to recreate and enjoy the dramatic effects of brave trees and plants atop stern mountain peaks, clinging to cliffs, or defying the elements raging around seaside boulders. These bonsai fall into two categories: those whose roots go from the stone on which the plant rests into the soil in the container below, and those whose roots do not. (The maple in the photographs illustrating repotting is an example of the former kind; see p. 39.)

Although it is sometimes claimed that bonsai with stones are impossible to raise in arid regions, as the photographs illustrate, with a little extra care and a few different steps, then can be successfully maintained. Generally, bonsai whose roots do not travel to the soil in the pot are set in a bed of sand on top of which water is poured.

Since the sunlight heats the rock on which the plants are set, root growth is usually very good and the plant is strong. In Japan, we use five-needle pines, Ezo spruce, two kinds of maple, juniper, and azaleas with small leaves for bonsai with stones. The plant shown in the second group of explanatory photographs is a five-needle pine.

**Tools Needed for Bonsai with Stones** (see p. 76)

   **a**  Turntable.
   **b**  Lead weights of the (Japanese) kind used in fishing (they should have holes through them).
   **c**  Copper wire.
   **d**  Bleached cotton or stainless-steel screening.
   **e**  Punch or a heavy-gauge nail.
   **f**  Hammer.
   **g**  Scissors for cutting away unwanted roots.
   **h**  Pincers.

**Selecting the Plant**

It is essential to allow the roots of plants destined for this kind of bonsai

to develop and grow fully. For this reason, they must be kept in fairly large preparations pots. We generally use rough-textured stones with irregular surfaces in these arrangements, which are usually found in the mountains, valleys, and dry river beds. Before placing the plant, decide whether you prefer a tall rising stone or a horizontally oriented one and examine it and the plant to determine the most balanced placement. Since once the plant is in place, it will not be moved for approximately ten years, take its growth into consideration by selecting a stone that is somewhat larger than you might feel is called for.

## Methods

❶ Cut the lead fishing weights in half, thread them on wires, and bend the wires in half at the centers, where the weight must be positioned.

❷ The lead pieces will be hammered into cracks in the stone at the points to which you want to attach the roots of the plant.

❸ In this photograph the wires and their lead weights have been hammered into place at the proper spots.

❹ The plant to be used is a five-needle pine.

❺ The roots must be as well developed as shown here.

❻ Make a trial placement of the plant on the stone.

❼ Soil. In Japan we generally use a *humus* of a kind similar to those found everywhere in the world. Knead it well and form it into balls.

❽ Press balls of kneaded *humus* into the crevices and openings in the stone.

❾ The stone filled with *humus*.

❿ Place one ball of *humus* on top of the rock at the place that will be directly under the trunk of the plant. This is similar to mounding the earth under the central part of plants at repotting time: it ensures that there is adequate soil in that important zone.

⓫ Decide on the final placement of the plant and fix it in place.

*Bonsai with Stones* **33**

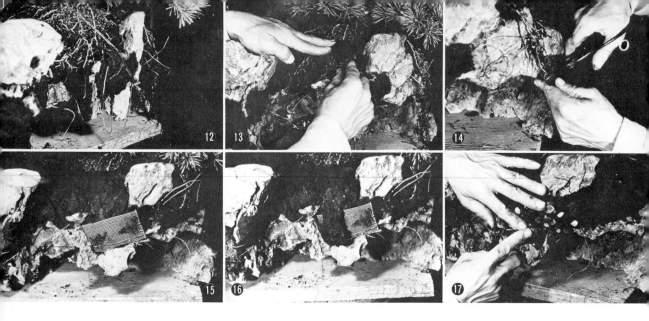

⑫   Spread the roots well. Use rubber pads to prevent the wire from touching the roots.

⑬   Next cover the roots well with *humus*.

⑭   Cut away unwanted roots.

⑮   To prevent the soil's dropping below the stone, hold it in place with a piece of bleached cotton, or a strip of screen net made of plastic or stainless steel.

⑯   Press *humus* into the screening.

⑰⑱   In this case miniature ivy is planted in the *humus* to keep the soil in place and to retain moisture.

⑲   The bonsai is complete.

⑳   It is next placed in a low flat container spread with sand and filled with water.

Both of these bonsai have remained as they were first set without alteration for ten years.

# 5. Group Planting

These photographs show an American bonsai training group who came to Japan to study.

In nature one more often encounters trees in groups than standing singly; for instance, the pine groves at the seaside or the stands of deciduous trees in the plains. Group planting is a way of capturing the feeling of such groves in bonsai terms. Generally select a shallow container that reveals the breadth and depth of the planting arrangement. If you will observe the following advise, you will always produce successful group-planting bonsai. Planting of the individual trees follows the same procedures used in repotting and in potting wild materials brought from forests and fields.

## Selecting the Trees

1.   Always choose a tree with good roots. You will be on the wrong track if you think that you may use a plant with roots spread in only one direction because all the plants are to be set in a group. Always choose a plant with a good spread of roots in all four directions and with no down-directed roots. If there are downward roots, you must cut them off close to the base of the plant.

2.   The plant must stand well. A plant that has been standing in a peculiar posture for two or three years, cannot be corrected. Consequently always select one with a good form. Some minor faults in the rest of the tree will do no harm; indeed, in combination with the other members of the group planting they might prove interesting.

3.   Selecting the main tree. The group should be varied in thickness and height of trunk. From them select the largest to be the main tree.

4.   Always plant in odd numbers. For the sake of balance and total appearance create groupings of three, five, or seven trees.

5.   Use a shallow container. A thin-rimmed oval container is easiest to deal with; it is very difficult to obtain proper balance and configuration in containers with right-angled corners.

## Caution Points in Planting

1.   Place the plants in a scalene triangle; that is, seen from above, they must assume this form.

2. Seen from the side, no tree should obstruct another.

3. For good placement, use the kind of perspective principles applied in painting.

4. Do not plant the main tree in the center of the container. It must be slightly to right or left of the center line leading from front to back and slightly in front of or behind the center line leading from side to side.

5. Mound the soil slightly under the main tree. This will be of great assistance in creating a sense of depth and composure.

6. Plant after spreading some slightly damp soil over the bottom of the container. This prevents the roots from drying out during the unavoidably lengthy period required to plant group bonsai and makes the planting itself easier: planting a number of trees in dry soil is very difficult.

7. Plant the main tree first.

8. Spread the roots of each tree to reach the edges of the container in all four directions.

9. To prevent the trees from toppling during planting, allow their branches to intertwine for support.

Anyone who follows these simple rules can create truly beautiful group planting bonsai. Almost any of the bonsai plants are suitable to this style, though flowering and fruit-bearing plants are especially interesting. I shall now give a few examples.

❶ Maples, the summer of their first year. I selected five of these and arranged them simply in a group planting. The two varieties of maple used in bonsai make excellent group arrangements. Planted together in a simple fashion, after four or five years, these maples will grow together to form one striking, multi-trunk tree.

❷ This photograph shows the trees three years after potting.

❸ This is the same tree ten years after potting. The root spread and the formation of the trunks are very handsome.

*Japanese Cypress Group Planting*

**❶** Materials. These cypress trees are from four to five years of age.

**❷** This grove of cypresses was planted in a shallow, oval container about two feet long four years ago. To increase its size and because I intended to transplant the group into another larger container in the future, I put the main tree a little close to center. This position would have been bad had I intended to leave the trees in this container for a long time.

**❸** Three years ago the group looked like this. The main tree is about one foot tall.

**❹** The group as it looked two years ago. Now about one and one-half feet tall, the main tree has a rich group of small branches, and the group has taken on the look of a real cypress grove.

**❺** The group as it looks today. It has been transplanted into a proper large container about three feet long. The position of the main tree has been altered. Eight trees have been added to the original group to make a total of thirty-five. Now the group truly gives the impression of a cypress gove.

**❻** The group seen from above. The small branches of the trees are developed in all four directions to resemble a grove in its natural state. This photograph gives one the feeling of looking down into a forest from an airplane.

# 6. Repotting

In general, deciduous and flowering and fruit-bearing trees exhaust the soil in their containers in about one year; pines and other evergreens do so in two or three years. When this happens, leaving the plants as they are without repotting them has dire effects on them. First of all the roots fill the pot and overlap in such a way as to spoil the drainage of the soil. This means that no matter how much one waters, the moisture never reaches the center of the root mass. Moreover, no amonut of fertilizing will do any good; in fact, it may well become the cause of root rot. The small rootlets wither, and other roots grow too thick. When this happens, branches tend to grow unevenly and irregularly, lower branches wither, leaves take on poor color and lose their vitality. Although the first purpose of repotting is to exchange good soil for the exhausted soil in the pot, it also provides a good opportunity for correcting the condition of the roots.

By cutting the old roots and thus stimulating the growth of many rootlets, one automatically stimulates the balanced growth of many small branches and the invigorating of all with the result that the entire form of the plant becomes lovelier.

Repot deciduous trees in the spring just before or just after they awaken from hibernation. As I shall point out later, pines and evergreens may be repotted somewhat later, even as late as midsummer.

## Repotting a Maple

Repot maples in the spring when the buds have just begun to swell. If not done then, repotting should be carried out after the leaves are out and firmly set. The tree in the photograph is an example of the latter. If the pot has not been neutralized, treat it ahead of time so that you may use it when needed.

❶ Cover the holes in the bottom of the container with stainless-steel mesh or plastic screen. In the photograph stainless steel is being used.

Ordinary iron or steel mesh may be used, but it rusts and soils the container holes. Since copper oxidizes and produces a substance harmful to the roots of plants it is not currently used in Japan.

**❷–❸** Tie a length of plastic-covered copper electric wire (1/64 or 1/32 inch in diameter) around a short length of thick copper or stainless wire. Both ends of the covered wire must be fairly long and of equal length. The thick wire will be placed under the container at the drainage hole, and the covered wires passed upward through the hole to be tied around and to hold the roots in place.

**❹** Once container preparations are finished, using a special scythe separate the soil mass from the container. Run the scythe around the edge but do not scratch the container. In the past, because of a lack of suitable tools, people frequently damaged valuable bonsai plants. But since, in recent years, the kind of scythe shown in the photograph has been on the market, this danger has greatly lessened.

**❺** Do not force the plant. Once it has been removed gently from its container, using either bamboo chopsticks or a bamboo spatula,

carefully remove the soil from among the roots.

**❻** Remove about one-third and leave about two-thirds of the soil.

**❼** Using sharp shears, trim off the roots so in such a way that their ends protrude slightly from the edge of the remaining soil mass. In order to ensure that the cuts face downward, always cut the roots on an angle from above.

**❽** The bottom of the root and soil mass.

**❾** Remove the soil from the bottom roots as well.

**❿** Trim away roots that have grown too long.

**⓫** In the bottom of the prepared pot spread a layer of gravelly soil.

**⓬** Spread a thin layer of potting soil over the gravelly layer. Mound it at the area that will be under the roots.

**⓭** Gently turning the plant from side to side to ensure the penetration of soil under the roots, position it in the correct part of the pot. Since you must be careful of both front-back and right-left placement while doing this, a turntable is very helpful.

⑭　Now gently tie the roots in place with the plastic covered wire you earlier inserted in the pot holes. Take care not to tie tightly as this will injure the roots. It has been recently discovered that in about three months after repotting the roots will bind themsleves to these wires either from above or below.

⑮　Tie the wires about as loosely as they appear in the photograph, but take care that they do not protrude above the top layer of soil. Cut off unwanted wire with wire cutters.

⑯　The tree tied in place.

⑰　Moving the chopsticks about, force soil gently among the root-lets; add a top coating that is somewhat thicker than will be wanted in the completed bonsai.

⑱　Press the soil around the base of the tree gently with the balls of the fingers. Since this is helpful in pressing that new soil among the roots it stimulates their activity and thus makes for a successful and effective repotting.

⑲　Brush away excess soil with a small hand broom.

⑳　Use a still smaller broom to get into small places.

㉑　Next press the surface of the soil with a trowel. The pressure applied varies with the kind of tree: slightly firm pressure for the evergreens and lighter pressure for deciduous trees. You will be better able

to judge the correct pressure from actual practice.

㉒　Press the soil down farther at the edges of the container.

㉓　Now that the repotting is finished, rotate the turntable once more for a final check. It is extremely difficult to repot a second time or make corrections after you have watered the repotted plant. Therefore, take a long slow look to make sure the front-back, right-left placement is satisfactory.

㉔　Now the watering. The flow from the watering can should be slanting and from the side. While rotating the turntable, water till the excess flows from the holes in the bottom of the container.

㉕　Finally, tilting the container, water the leaves thoroughly.

㉖　Now that it has been repotted, set the plant on a suitable table and admire it. In this case, changing the maple to a more harmonious container has greatly enhanced its loveliness. For about three weeks after repotting exercise great care that the plant is not subject to winds, that it receives sufficient water, and that the soil in the pot does not dry out. As a rule for plants repotted in the spring, plenty of sunlight stimulates growth. Do not fertilize for at least two weeks after repotting for if you do so prematurely it may seriously damage the plant. At repotting time, one usually corrects any bad aspects of the form of the tree, but since this maple was well shaped, this step was unnecessary.

## Repotting a Five-needle Pine

Repotting a five-needle pine is, in fact, not very different from the procedure for any other tree, except that the mixture of white mould that grows with the roots improves the general effectiveness of the operation. Mixing this white mould with the soil used for old pines is often especially effective. Although once in four or five years is frequent enough, some think that a yearly replanting improves pines. Moreover, since no specially difficult care is needed after repotting, many bonsai fanciers now repot this often. In the past, it was thought best to repot five-needle pines in early April when the buds first become active, but since the Japanese weather is unsettled at that time and tends to sudden cold snaps which damage the buds, for the past twenty years or so, cultivators have been waiting somewhat longer. It is now thought best to transplant either in late June, when the needles have come out and show their five-position placement, or even from late August to late September when the needles are firmly set. At this time, in Japan at any rate, the moisture in the air is more or less stable, and the white mould that grows among the pine roots is most active. Moreover, the activity of the tree is very rapid for a period of one week to ten days; therefore, there is less danger of branches' withering. Although all of the pines can stand very little damage to their roots, at this later season, they produce a resin that heals slight root cuts and thus prevents branches from dying.

❶ This five-needle pine, whose roots are in good condition, is to be repotted in the same container. The first step is to use wire clippers to cut the covered wire holding the tree in place.

❷ Run a removal scythe around the edge of the soil and root mass as you did for the maple in the preceding section.

❸ Remove the root and soil mass taking great care that the covered wire is not jerked or pulled in such a way as to damage the roots.

❹ Examine the bottom of the root and soil mass. The spots of white mould on the bottom are a kind of barometer of the health of the tree.

❺ Remove the areas in which the white mould is specially plentiful of course you may use white mould cultivated by some other five-needle pine as well—and sift it.

❻ The sifted mould.

❼ Pinch up some of the mould and sprinkle it on the bottom of the container. Mix some more with the new potting soil.

❽–❾ Trim the roots as you did for the maple in the preceding section.

❿ Use sharp shears (No. 128. see p. 79.) and cut so that the open ends of the trimmed roots face down. This is necessary to prevent water from entering the wounds and to stimulate the growth of rootlets.

⓫ The tree after the roots have been trimmed. It is customary to trim the roots of the bottom of the mass at this time. Judge whether to take this step by examining the bottom of the root-soil mass.

⓬ Spread a layer of gravelly soil on the bottom of the container.

⓭ Cover this with a layer of potting soil; then position the tree by pressing it as you determine the best placement. In the photograph, excess soil has been swept away to make this explanation clear. Remember to mix the white mould with the potting soil before putting it in the container.

⓮ Since the tree is large, it is necessary to tie the covered wires above the surface of the root mass. In about three months after repotting, the wires above the ground may be cut off. The underground ones will be left as they are.

⓯–⓰ After putting in a small amount of soil sprinkle it with some white mould.

⓱ Top this with potting soil.

⓲ Working gently and taking care to be very thorough, press soil among the roots with chopsticks.

⓳ After this process is finished, press the soil between the base of the plants and the section of new soil with the balls of the fingers. Press stronger for pines than for deciduous trees.

⓴ Using a fairly large brush, sweep away the soil clinging to the base of the tree.

**㉑** Now with a hand broom brush the soil till it is even.

**㉒** Sweep away all the coarser particles leaving the finer ones on the surface.

**㉓** Press the surface of the soil with a trowel.

**㉔** Depending on the location, press with different parts of the trowel blade to produce the desired smooth effect.

Repotting tools.

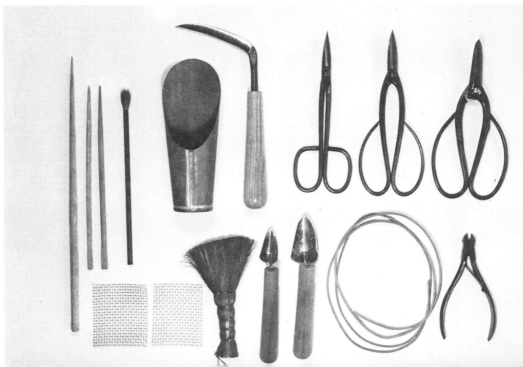

㉕　As you did with the maple, press the areas adjacent to the edge of the container to make them low and rounded.

㉖–㉘　Water following the procedures used with the maple.

㉙　For the first week after repotting, do not allow rain to fall on the pine and water adequately but with moderation.

For five-needled and black pines and other trees that produce a white mould with the rootlets, water in the morning. By evening the surface of the soil will be slightly dry. This set of circumstances facilitates the growth of the mould. The care of these trees after repotting is very easy: all one need do is assure adequate moisture, and they will recover with great speed.

# 7. Trimming Buds

This is the first and one of the most important ways of correcting a bonsai shape. By concentrating the strength of the young bud, trimming it prevents branches that run too long and promotes the growth of short small, luxuriant branches. Consequently bud trimming is one of the best ways to make a bonsai look like a tree in its natural setting. The species of plant determines the season in which to trim buds. Furthermore, in some trees one trimming is all that is needed, whereas in others the process must be repeated time and time again. There are a number of ways of trimming buds.

### 1. Pines
One may keep pine bonsai branches short by cutting off some of the needles of a fresh bud shoot with a sharp pair of bud-trimming scissors. In addition, trimming causes new small branches to develop at the base of the treated bud (Photographs ❶ and ❷).

### 2. Ezo spruce, cedar, juniper
These buds should be plucked with the fingers when they first appear.

### 3. Oak, cypress
Using the fingertips, pluck only the core of the bud; one must not remove too much.

In cases of the trees listed in 2 and 3 never use scissors. Instead always pluck with the fingertips as shown in Photographs ❸ and ❹.

4. *Usually buds of fruit-bearing bonsai are not trimmed.*
If a particular bud runs to too great a length it may be cut. Irregular buds sometimes appear. These may be trimmed off as necessary.

5. *Maples, zelkova, elm, etc.*
Since these trees bud from spring into summer, they may be trimmed fairly severely; remove all but two base leaves from each cluster. Do not remove buds that appear after autumn has begun.

6. Always remember that buds turned upward and the growing power of the top of the plant are stronger than downward turned buds or the ends of lower branches. If you forget this and trim all buds to the same degree, you can easily spoil the shape of the tree (Photograph ❺).

**Bud-trimming scissors.**
The considerable opening between the handles prevents injuring other buds. These scissors are used for pines and other trees. Never use them to cut hard woody branches. The scissors come in large and small sizes. The large size opens wider.

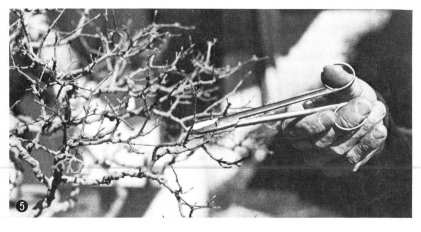

# 8. Trimming Leaves

The purpose of this step is to force the plant to put out two years' growth of small branches in the span of one year. It can be successfully performed on plants that continually put out buds from spring till early autumn: maples, zelkova, etc. Though it is uncertain when the practice began, our forefathers, observing the characteristics of certain plants, devised this way of enhancing the appearance of decidous bonsai.

### 1. Maples
Once the new leaves are out and well set, cut the small branches about midway between clusters of leaves as shown in the photograph. This is more conveniently done with shears. As you see, buds will emerge from the cut place.

### 2. Zelkova, beech, etc.
When the new leaves are out and firmly set, trim off some leaves at their bases. The elm trees may have their leaves trimmed twice in one year.

### 3. Points for special caution
Since this process causes a subdivision of the small branches it imposes a considerable burden on the tree. Do not use it on weak or very old plants or on weak branches.

### 4. Order for trimming leaves
After June—maples, zelkova and elm, and finally beech in the summer.

**❶** Holding the shears, with maples cut midway the leaf stem.

**❷** Holding the shears.

**❸** After leaf trimming.

**❹** Three weeks after leaf trimming. Buds are appearing from the place on the leaf stem were trimming was performed.

**❺** Using a woodcarving knife or other similar tool cut irregular buds as quickly as they appear.

# 9. Pruning

Pruning, which is of the greatest importance, requires the greatest of care. One must not merely snip branches here and there at random. The nature goddess's wonderful skill produces the ineffably beautiful forms of trees in their natural state, and we, understanding the characters of the plants we deal with, can produce something approaching this beauty in bonsai. In a natural state, in order to assure adequate sunlight and good ventilation, the trees themselves extend branches they need and allow to wither and drop others that are either useless or harmful. The beautiful shapes of natural trees are the result of this natural kind of adjustment.

## The Basic Purpose of Pruning

Ideally sunlight will reach all branches equally. When this state is attained, proper ventilation will follow inevitably. Finally, under these conditions, the form of the plant will resemble that of a natural tree. Always remember these basic purposes when pruning.

## Season for Pruning

Pruning for all deciduous plants takes place before the buds become active in the spring.

1. Prune most deciduous trees for repotting before the buds become active in the spring.

2. Prune these when the flowers have bloomed and dropped—plum, azalea.

3. Prune these before they begin to hibernate—pines (black pine, red pine, five-needle pine, and *nishiki* pine).

4. Prune these for the sake of adjusting the number of blossoms in the autumn before they begin hibernating—flowering plants such as the plum and the quince.

5. Prune these during winter hibernation—Ezo spruce, juniper, pine, cypress, larch.

### Pruning Scissors

**❶**   These scissors will cut branches that are usually considered too thick for scissors or shears. They are capable of cutting through a branch with a diameter half as thick as the blade of the scissors are long. They combine the cutting and the smoothing operation in one movement and are available in two sizes to suit the thicknesses of the branches to be cut.

**❷**   Since the blades are slanted it is possible to cut branches located deep within the plant and to cut at many different angles.

**❸–❺**   Medium pruning shears. Use these to cut excessively long branches that have already developed a woody substance. It is also possible to use them in bud-trimming and in cutting branches as thick as one- fourth the length of the blades.

**❻–❼**   This knot cutter can be used for cutting small knots or branches and for cutting a trunk perfectly flat. They are also useful in smoothing wounds. They come in large and small sizes.

### Pruning during Growth

This is limited to branches that run too long and distorted branches. These must be cut from the base of the branch. But even in these cases, during the growth season, trim long or distorted branches lightly. It is necessary to wait until the spring, before the buds become active, to cut these branches off at their bases.

### Pruning at Repotting Time

*1.   Roots*

Repotting time is a good season for pruning. When cutting roots that

have grown too long, one must take the moisture balance into consideration and cut a proportionate amount of branches as well. Unnatural growth in bonsai branches can result from overlooking this principle. Though it may seem surprising, in fact, roots cause a large percentage of irregular unsightly bonsai growth.

Senior bonsai cultivators of many years' experience are said to be able to tell the state of a plant's roots from the appearance of its branches. If the roots are greatly twisted and distorted, the branches will not grow properly; if the roots are piled one on another, distorted branches will develop; if one root is disproportionately thick, the branches too will be out of balance. From this, one can see that no amount of pruning of branches will correct the shape of a tree whose roots are in bad condition; sooner or later it will revert to its bad shape.

The important thing in pruning roots is to create a good spread in four directions. Repotting is an excellent chance to do this. Cut the tips of roots that are too thick. Central thick roots must be cut straight across at their bases. In these cases it is not necessary to retrim the root cuts after pruning. If you are careful to cut smoothly the first time. and if you use sharp root-pruning shears in the size (large or small) that suits the root that must be cut (see p. 76).

Trim roots that are too long by evening the root mass. In potting, be sure to straighten out roots that are twisted or bent. Plant the tree so that the fine roots at the base of the trunk are exposed to plenty of sunlight for this will help them thicken. Conversely, until the thin roots at the base have grown to the desired thickness, cover thick roots with moss to prevent their growing thicker.

Cut out roots that have overlapped. When all this is done, root pruning is finished.

a. branches thrusting
too far in one direction

b. standing branches

c. backward bent branches

d. branches thrusting forward

### 2. *Branches*

Prune any of the following so-called objectionable branches.

    a. branches thrusting too far in one direction
    b. standing branches
    c. backward bent branches
    d. branches thrusting forward
    e. unsightly twisted branches
    f. branches bent into near circles
    g. branches forked at the same level
    h. axial branches
    i. frog-leg branches
    j. parallel branches
    k. dropped branches

When it is desirable to cut a trunk perfectly flat, use a knot cutter. If it is too large for a knot cutter use root sheers. When it is necessary to cut a branch flat at the base use branch shears.

To cut a branch off smooth at the trunk so that the bark will cover it quickly, use a chisel or a woodcarving knife. Branches are generally trimmed in an order beginning at the lower reaches and moving upward in a spiral around the tree. Once again, it is important to remember what I said about comparative growing strengths of the upper and lower parts of the tree (see p. 49). The moisture must be kept in balance with pruning. With a little practice, however, anyone can learn to do this. It is easy to recognize a tree that is in good condition. A look at any collection of famous bonsai, or any exhibition, or a trip to the nursery of an established bonsai cultivator will show how indescribably lovely is a tree with a good four-directional roots spread, a fine rising posture, and good branches that are well placed. Observing as many fine bonsai as possible is one shortcut to successful cultivation. Watch the models carefully and keep in mind the advice I have given in this section. Although I am repeating myself it is worthwhile saying again that a person who carefully trains the root masses always produces good bonsai shapes. The relationship between roots and shape are rarely treated in bonsai books, but I hope my reader will remain conscious of its importance.

e. unsightly twisted branches

f. branches bent
into near circles

g. branches forked
at the same level

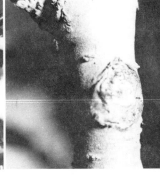

**1** Branches doubling back on a trunk may be pruned with a knot cutter.

**2** Irregular buds that have reached the stage they are difficult to snip off may be removed with a knot cutter.

**3** The flat place where a branch has been removed at the base with a knot cutter.

**4** When three branches fork at the same level, cut out the middle one at the base with a fork-branch cutter.

**5** The place from which the center of a triple fork branch was removed.

**6** A so-called dropped branch.

**7** Intersecting branches. One of them must be removed with a knot cutter.

**8** A branch that bends back on the trunk.

**9** This must be removed with a fork-branch cutter.

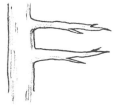

h.  axial branches       i.  frog-leg branches       j.  parallel branches       k.  dropped branches

# 10. Root Renewal

As I said in the chapter on pruning, a four direction root spread is the bonsai ideal. If the tree that does not meet this requirement is old, pruning is the only thing that can be done, but if it is young and healthy and if it belongs to one of the species that lend themselves to a technique known as layering, it is possible to produce a new bonsai from it with a perfect four-directional root spread. In the following paragraphs I give some examples of ways in which this can be done.

## Circle Bark Stripping

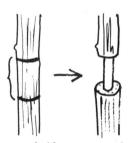

one-half times as wide as the diameter

After examining a certain branch and deciding that if roots could be produced from it the results would be a good four-directional spread, using a sharp knife, make two incisions around the branch. The cuts must outline a strip about one and one-half times as wide as the diameter of the branch at that point and must extend to the woody part of the tree. Peel the bark as you do in preparing a *jin* (see p. 60). If you leave the growth layer, which is the part of the plant that produces leaves and that descends all the way to the roots, it will grow a new bark covering, and your effort in peeling will have been wasted. For this reason it is essential to peel away everything to the woody part of the branch.

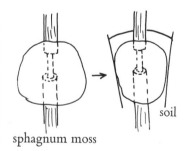

sphagnum moss

When this process is complete, wrap the peeled section in sphagnum moss to a thickness of three times the diameter of the branch. Plant this in a pot deep enough to cover the peeled area and its moss completely in soil. In about one month roots should generate from the peeled zone. After the roots are well out and the time for transplanting has passed, remove the plant and using root-cutting shears, cut off the part below the newly generated roots. The cut must go straight across the trunk. After gently and carefully removing the sphagnum moss, repot according to the standard procedure. The period that must lapse before repotting varies with the species.

**Cutting the roots.** Unwanted roots that thrust upward through the soil may be cut off at soil level.

### Layering with Wire

Wrap wire so tightly that it cuts into the bark at the place from which you want the roots to generate and bury the plant deep as in the preceding method. When the new roots are out and well spread, repot.

### Times for Layering and Potting

Generally speaking the period from spring into summer is considered optimum for these operations, but it differs slightly with the kind of plant being treated. Nevertheless, if one selects late spring the chances for success with most trees are good.

Plants that may be potted in from two to three months after layering include azaleas, maples, pyracantha, oak, cedar, pomegranate, and zelkova. Those that require from three to six months are the black pine and the rhododendron. Plants that must wait for from six months to a year before being potted include the Ezo spruce as well as a few others. When layering has been slightly late with the result that the proper time for potting will come in cold weather, one is safer waiting until the following spring.

# 11. The Jin

I shall now turn to that striking and stark withered, sometimes dead looking part of those mighty old trees whose strength and endurance have seen them through centuries of snows and winds and the buffetings of the natural elements. This part is called the *jin*. Natural *jin* result when lightning strikes a tree and kills a branch, when strong winds break a branch, or when a branch naturally dies and withers to the bone-white of exposed wood. These natural *jin* frequently occur in wild materials brought from the mountains or the forests. In the following sections I shall explain ways of perfecting an incomplete *jin* in a natural plant, of preserving a branch or trunk tip that withered in bonsai cultivation and making of it an asset instead of a liability, as well as other ways of producing in bonsai the appearance of the natural *jin*.

The following are some examples of outstanding *jin*-style bonsai.

Ⓐ A *shinpaku* (Chinese juniper) with a natural *jin* in the form of a withered trunk tip.

Ⓑ *Tosho* (needle juniper) with a whitened trunk and a *jin* on a branch.

❶ The branch shown died during cultivation. To cut it off would be to sadden the appearance of the tree greatly; therefore, I will leave it on but convert it into a *jin*.

❷ The first step is to make incisions at the area from which the bark is to be stripped.

❸ If the incision extends to the woody part of the branch the bark can be removed very easily.

❹ Continuing making incisions and removing bark along the length of the branch.

❺ In this instance it is a good idea to make the opposite branch a *jin* too.

**❻–❽**  Strip the bark from the end of the branch to complete the *jin*.

**❾–❿**  In this case the branch is already quite dead, consequently it is impossible to strip the wood away to the woody layer as was done in the preceding, all one can do is to use a woodcarving knife and carefully cut away all remaining bits of bark.

**⓫**  Be sure to remove all of the bark, even that deep in the natural grooves of the branch.

**⓬**  Once the bark is entirely removed the *jin* is complete except for final smoothing with sand paper.

⓭     Branch *jin* in a Ezo spruce.
⓮     Branch *jin* in a needle juniper.

### Tools Needed for *Jin* Preparation (see p. 76)

    **a**    turntable.
    **b**    piece of blanket.
    **c**    rubber strips.
    **d**    woodcarving knives.
    **e**    a group of different sizes of rounded gouges.
    **f**    hammer.
    **g**    saw.
    **h**    sandpaper.

### *Jin* on trunks

❶    A two-trunk needle juniper pine brought from the mountains and potted. The completely dead trunk on the right was too long. It was trimmed diagonally with a saw.

❷    This must be placed on a turntable since the bark must be cut away as the tree rotates.

❸    To protect the container from falling tools, wrap it in an old blanket, which must extend well above the base of the tree.

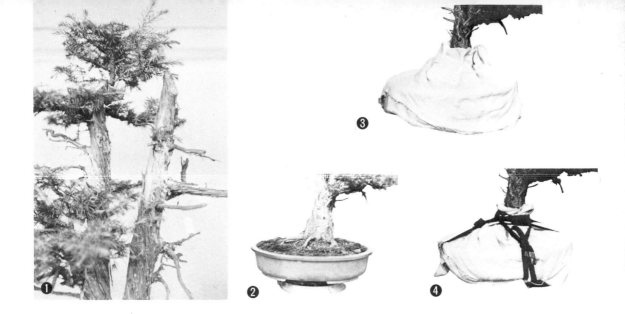

❹ Fix the blanket in place with strips of rubber—from an inner tube—before beginning operations.

❺ Gradually cut away the end of the trunk with a rounded gouge. Use a hammer to tap the gouge for the first rough carving. Be careful to make the cuts look as natural as possible.

❻ Perform the finer carving with sharp woodcarving knives and finish with sandpaper.

❼ The *jin* is complete when it looks as natural as this. As you see, anyone with the proper tools can make a *jin*-style bonsai. The tree need not have a naturally withered part. In fact, it is easier to make a *jin* from a living branch. The *jin* adds greatly to the dignity and drama of a bonsai.

**❶** Trimming a withered branch into a *jin*.

**❷** Cleaning bark from a groove in a *jin* by pulling the tool forward.

**❸** Cleaning a deep groove in a *jin*.

**❹** Carving an addition groove.

**❺** Removing bits of bark from a deep groove in a *jin*.

# 12. Wiring

Wiring, the purpose of which is to alter the shapes of branches and trunk in order to bring them as close as possible to the bonsai ideal, is the most attention- and skill-demanding of all bonsai techniques. The effects of wiring may be divided into the following three major categories.

1. To preserve the present shape for many years.
2. To produce a different form by altering the old one of the plant.
3. To create a totally new form.

The first method is used year in year out on the small branches of almost all completed bonsai. The second is used only when the cultivator is sufficiently displeased with the old form of the plant and is convinced that by correcting it he can make something much better. The technique is difficult and often leads to failure; consequently, it requires the closest attention and the most sophisticated skills. The third method is used on plants raised from seedlings and cuttings. Although it looks easy at a glance, in fact it too requires considerable experience.

Since Kyuzo Murata in his *Bonsai* of 1964 has already explained selection of kind and thickness of wire and the periods that must elapse before the wire can be removed, I will here deal only with a chart explanation of the basics of wrapping the wire and with the kinds of tools used in applying and removing the wire from trunks and branches.

❶ Hodling the end of the wire firmly in place, wrap it loosely around the branch or trunk.

❷ When a severe bend is needed, hold the plant as shown and bend the branch gently. The wire must cross on top of the bend.

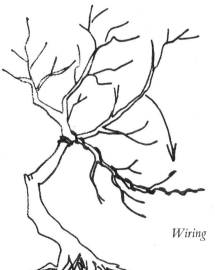

❸ The arrow indicates the direction in which the branch must bend.

**❶ Using the wire cutters (No.108).** Used for cutting copper wire of less than 3/32 inch diameter.

**❷ Holding and using small wire cutters.** Used for cutting wire of less than 1/8 inch, these cutters may be held by the middle finger inserted in the handle.

**❸ Using pincers (No. 18).** Large ones for bending wire of above 5/32 of an inch in diameter small ones for wire of less than 1/8 of an inch.

# 13 . Watering and Positioning

Ideally bonsai should be kept in a place with good ventilation and good sun, but with not too much western sun. The best way to keep a bonsai with stones is to make a large basin of concrete, spread sand in the bottom of it, fill it water, and place the bonsai on a platform in it. The stones in these arrangements get hot in the summer sun and could cause the plant to dessicate dangerously, but evaporation from the water in the basin below helps maintain a certain amount of moisture.

❶ Placing bonsai by a body of water where the sun, shining on the water, reflects on the undersides of the leaves greatly promotes growth.
❷ Recently large shelves in the garden for bonsai, which then become a semi-interior ornament, have become popular. The shelves and stands should be about three feet tall for easy watering.

**❸–❺**  In watering, be sure to use a nozzle with a very fine spray. Never train a powerful stream of water on the soil for this washes it away. Instead water from all four sides and from a distance that allows the water just to reach the container and soil. The photographs give a good idea of a proper shelf arrangement as well as of the correct way to water.

# 14. Using Bonsai Tools

## Proper Ways to Hold Tools

If you do not hold a golf club properly and assume the correct posture when you swing, the ball will not go where you want it to. Just as the clubs are tailored to the needs of golf, so bonsai tools are specially designed and have very subtle cutting actions requiring correct grip and way of use. Some bonsai scissors and cutters may be held by inserting either one or two fingers in the handle. Others require the strength and grip of the whole hand, for instance forked-branch cutters and knot cutters. Other still heavier tools require the firm grip of both hands.

## Breaking in

A new automobile or a new machine of any kind requires breaking in; so do bonsai tools. One must not attempt to cut heavy or hard branches and trunks with a pair of newly bought shears or cutters. They must be broken in first. The best way to do this is to cut grassy plants. About fifty cuts of stalks of some grass will align the blades of cutters and scissors correctly. You may also use newspaper for this purpose. Fold the paper into eight thicknesses and make about fifty break-in cuts.

## Accurate Cutting

Use the same amount of pressure and the same grip from the beginning to the end of a single cut. Never change either during the cut.

## Cut Straight Across a Branch Only When Absolutely Necessary

Bud-trimming shears are designed to be used on tender young greenery. They must never be used to cut woody branches or the dead

Curved tweezrs

Tweezers with spatula end

Wire cutters

ends of branches. Furthermore, avoid using them in cutting straight across a bud. Even ordinary pruning shears should not be used to cut straight across a branch unless it is absolutely unavoidable. The ideal angle for cutting is about forty-five degrees. If you must use shears for a straight-across cut, hold the branch in one hand and, gripping the scissors correctly, rotate them downwards as you cut. Simultaneously, press the branch in a downward direction. This method requires only one-third of the grip power that would be otherwise needed. Only knot cutters, root cutters, and fork-branch cutters may be safely used in cutting either at angles or straight across.

### Position of Blade Contact

Pruning-shear blades are long; consequently, one must alter the spot of contact between branch and blade in accordance with the thickness of the material being pruned. For instance, cut only very thin branches and buds with the tips of the blades, and use the heavier part of the blades nearer the base for larger material. Maximum thickness for branches to be cut with No. 1 shears is about the size of the little finger. Shears No. 2 and No. 28 will cut branches as thick as a pencil (see p. 76–77).

### Never Wrench Shears and Cutters

Of course this is true of all scissors, but one must never wrench shears during cutting for this throws the blades out of line and spoils the cutting condition of delicately balanced tools. For instance, sometimes in using knot cutters or root cutters on material thicker than the width of the blades, it happens that although one blade comes free from the material, one remains embedded in it. If you wrench or twist the blade in such an instance it is certain to break. Instead, moving the blade parallel to its own direction right and left very slowly, gradually free it from the wood. Cutters of these two varieties virtually never break in the cutting process, but one must be very careful in removing them from woody substances.

### Beware of Foreign Matter

Always carefully remove small pieces of stone, gravel, or sand that might cling to branches before cutting. These small pieces of foreign matter can ruin the condition of perfectly good tools. Of course, if the ends of wired branches must be cut, remove the wire beforehand.

## Use Tools That Suit the Work to Be Done

There are many kinds of bonsai tools designed to meet all the needs of cultivation and training; therefore, do not cause yourself needless trouble by trying to make to do with a minimum. Selecting the right tools for the right job is the secret to the creation of beautiful bonsai.

## Care after Use

With a little post-use care, bonsai tools will keep their edges for many years without sharpening. The maintenance methods are extremely simple and easy; put them to immediate and sustained practice from the moment you buy a new bonsai tool.

1. First of all wipe off moisture and dirt with a cloth.
2. Take care to wipe off all tree sap from the cutting edges and their undersides. This is especially easy to do if the shears or cutters are shiny and new. If the sap is difficult to remove, breathe on the blades before wiping. Neglecting to take this step leads directly to rusting. Of course, the quality of the steel, the level of technology used in production, and the completeness of the tempering determine the cutting performance of these tools, but rust can ruin even the finest shears. Sometimes rust that is invisible to the naked eye can work great harm; consequently, it is wise to prevent trouble by careful wiping and drying.
3. Removing difficult stains
If breathing on the blade and wiping fail to do the trick, gently scrape away the stain with a bamboo or wooden spatula. Follow this with a good wiping with benzene or some other volatile spirit.
4. Oiling
After removing all the sap and other stains from the blades, oil them and the handles as well with some rust-preventing oil.

Tools subjected to this simple post-use care will last even a bonsai specialist who uses them everyday, about three years.

## Treatment for Rusted Tools

In the case of light rust, simple removal of the rust will put the tool back into good working condition. In most scissors the steel section is welded at the underside of the blade; the steel ranges from about one-third to one-fifth the thickness of the head. It is clearly visible as a band about one-sixteenth of an inch on the upper side of the blade. You can clearly tell which is steel and which is the basic iron structure of tools when they rust, because the colors of the rust on the two metals

A small hand-broom

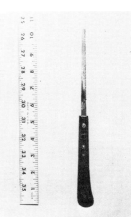

A hand-saw

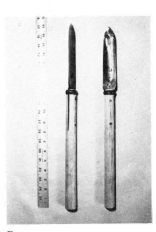

Root cutters

differ. Following the procedure explained below, polish just the steel part on either a water- or oil-lubricated whetstone.

**Polishing**

If the rust is serious or if the shears are out of alignment, they must be polished by a professional. Furthermore, if the undersides of the blades are badly rusted nothing can be done to restore the tool.

1. *Oil-lubricated whetstone*
   a.   Open the scissors so that one blade is fully exposed.
   b.   Hold the blade to be polished on a rigid surface.
   c.   Holding the whetstone in your hand, apply kerosene to it and press it to the blade in such a way that the stone conforms to the shape of the blade surface. The section of the blade must look like that in Fig. 1. Scissor blades must never be polished to a sharp point as shown in Fig. 2.
   d.   When a small amount of cutting edge appears in the underside, the upper side of the blade is finished. That is, when touched the underside of the cutting edge should seem somewhat sharp.
   e.   Never polish the underside of the blade. If the edge seems uniformly sharp, that is enough.

2. *Water-lubricated whetstone*
   In this case, the stone is held fixed and the blade is moved.
   a.   Hold the whetstone firmly on a flat surface.
   b.   Open the scissors so that one blade is completely exposed. Move this blade back and forth over the stone, the as surface of which must be kept wet at all times.
   c.   Judge whether the edge is sharp in the same way as for blades polished on an oil-lubricated whetstone.

If the blades of a tool are more than one-eighth of an inch out of alignment, an amateur cannot repair them. Unfortunately, the best thing to do in such cases is to buy a new pair.

Please use your tools as I have suggested and take care of them. If we suppose that mute plants have some kind of feeling, being pruned with dull ill-conditioned tools must be painful to them. On the other hand, if the shears and cutters you use are sharp and well cared for you will find that budding is more vigorous, roots will be healthier, and the wounds made in cutting will heal faster. In short, care of tools is one of the bonsai cultivator's duties.

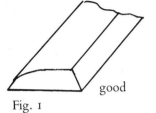
Fig. 1   good

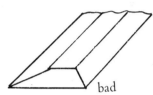
Fig. 2   bad

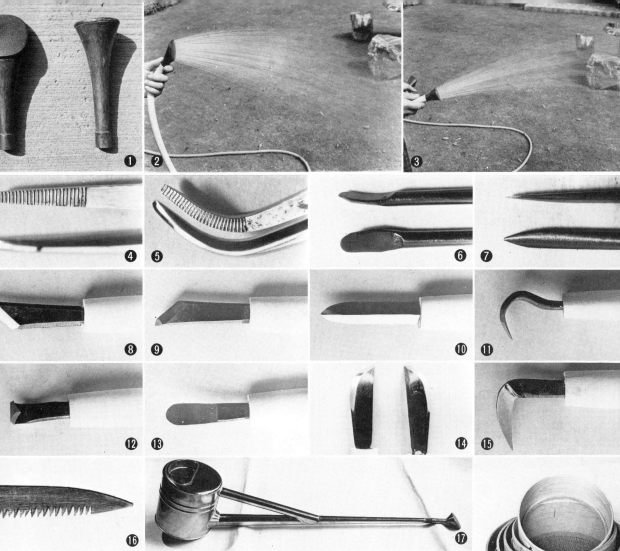

## Tools

**1**   Watering nozzles: left—fine mist; right—ordinary spray.

**2**   Nozzle in use; the fine mist spray.

**3**   Ordinary spray. Forceful sprays like this are unsuitable for use on freshly repotted plants.

**4**   Ends of a pair of No. 11 pincettes (see p. 76). The corrugation prevents buds from slipping out of the pincettes during trimming.

**5**   Ends of a pair of No. 27 curved pincettes (see p. 76).

**6**   Insect-removing probes. In addition to the use expressed in their name, these tools are useful for removing irregular buds.

**7**   Top and side view of insect-removing probes.

**8**–**15**   Woodcarving tools.

**16**   Saw.   **17**   Watering nozzle.   **18**   Sieves.

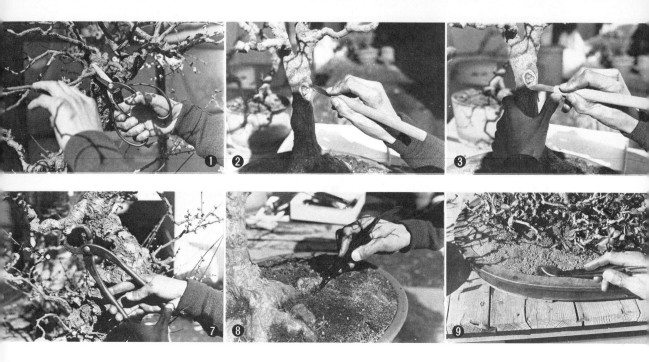

Holding scissors correctly

## Using Tools

❶ Pruning shears—When cutting off fairly thick branches—about the size of the little finger—hold the branch in one hand and press it downward slightly to facilitate the operation.

❷ Woodcarving knife (right blade)—Used here to trim the edge of a cut wound to speed the growth of a cover of bark and thus to make the wound inconspicuous.

❸ Woodcarving knife (left blade)—Used again to trim the edge of a wound.

❹ Woodcarving knife—Curved blade.

❺ Root cutter (large) These are useful in removing unsightly thick roots at repotting time and in cutting off unwanted roots and knots from newly acquired wild material. They can remove knots from other trees and can be used in cutting pine branches partially for bending.

❻ These cutters can be used to cut knots and branches thicker than the cutter blades are wide if repeated cuts are made. But when this is done, though one blade comes out of the wood easily, the other may remain imbedded, In such cases do not wrench the tool; instead remove it gently gradually shifting it from side to side in a direction parallel to that of the imbedded blade.

❼　Small root cutters used when large ones are not essential.

❽　Pincettes can be used for plucking out weeds and grasses that spring up in bonsai pots.

❾　The spatula head of the pincettes is useful for pressing moss into place.

❿　They may also be used to remove moss.

⓫　Pincettes are helpful in pressing soil in place after repotting.

⓬　Curved pincettes will remove unwanted buds from places where straight pincettes cannot go.

⓭　They help remove flowers that are too numerous.

⓮　This pair of pincettes is a labor saving device for the removal of spider webs that turn up in bonsai with great frequency.

⓯　Insect-removing probes are excellent for getting rid of the scale insects that often plague bonsai.

⓰　This rounded-edge trowel is indipsensable for pressing into a smooth surface the soil in a round edge container.

⓱　The flat back edge of the trowel too is useful.

⓲　And for square and rectangular containers, the flat edge of the trowel is required.

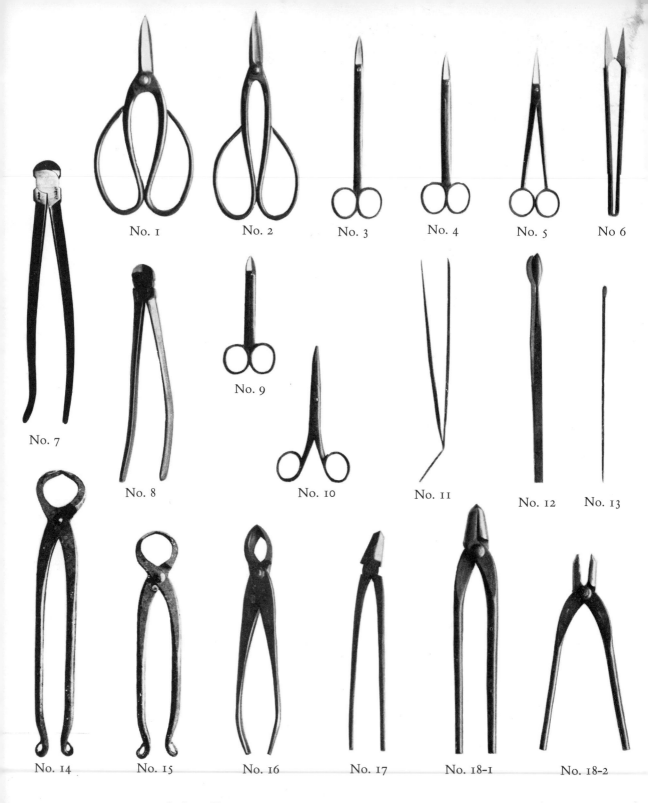

No. 1

No. 2

No. 3

No. 4

No. 5

No 6

No. 7

No. 8

No. 9

No. 10

No. 11

No. 12

No. 13

No. 14

No. 15

No. 16

No. 17

No. 18-1

No. 18-2

### Tools for All Bonsai Needs

No. 1 Trimming shears
No. 2 Trimming shears
with long handle
No. 3 Bud-trimming shears,
large
No. 4 Bud-trimming shears,
small

No. 5 Bud-trimming shears
for pine
No 6 Shears for leaf
trimming
No. 7 Wire cutters KYUKA
type, large
No. 8 Wire cutters KYUKA

type, small
No. 9 Wire cutters
No. 10 Wire remover
No. 11 Tweezer with spatula
end
No. 12 Tweezers for
removing spiders

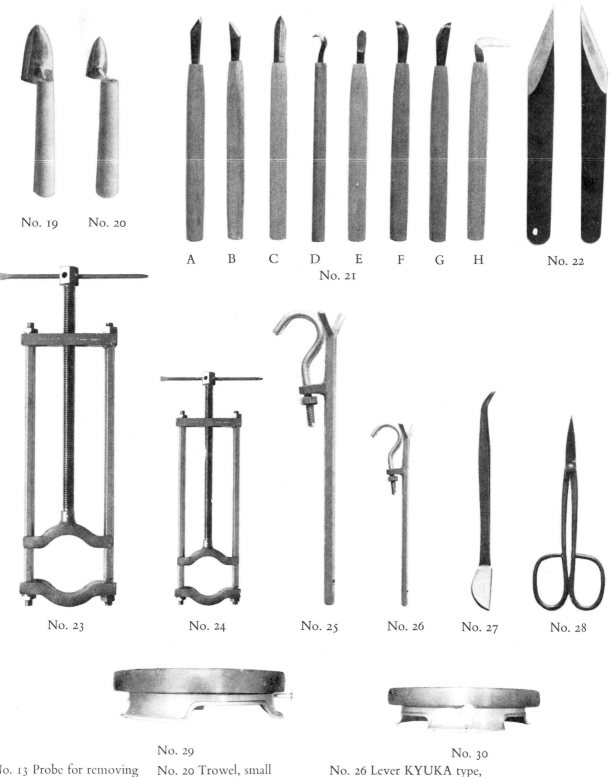

No. 19    No. 20

A  B  C  D  E  F  G  H    No. 22

No. 21

No. 23    No. 24    No. 25    No. 26    No. 27    No. 28

No. 29           No. 30

No. 13 Probe for removing insects
No. 14 Root cutters, large
No. 15 Root cutters, small
No. 16 Nippers for twigs
No. 17 Nipper for *Jin* preparation
No. 18-1 Nippers
No. 18-2 Nippers
No. 19 Trowel, large

No. 20 Trowel, small
No. 21 Wood-carving knives
No. 22 Grafting knife
No. 23 Jack KYUKA type, large
No. 24 Jack KYUKA type, small
No. 25 Lever KYUKA type, large

No. 26 Lever KYUKA type, small
No. 27 Curved tweezers
No. 28 Trimming shears, medium
No. 29 Turn table with stopper, large
No. 30 Turn table with stopper, small

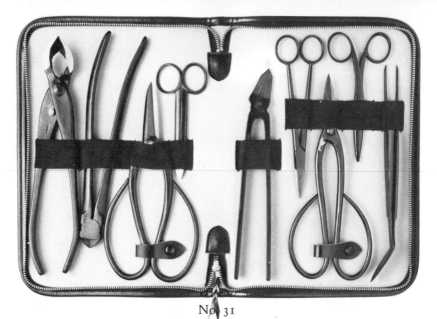

No. 31

**The Masakuni Bonsai set used by Their Imperial Majesties the Emperor and Empress of Japan.**

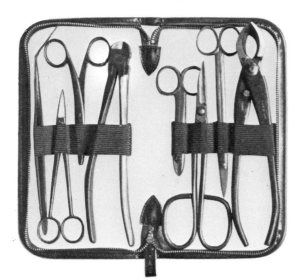

No. 32

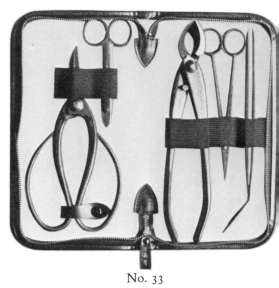

No. 33

No. 34

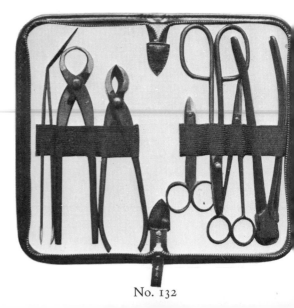

No. 132

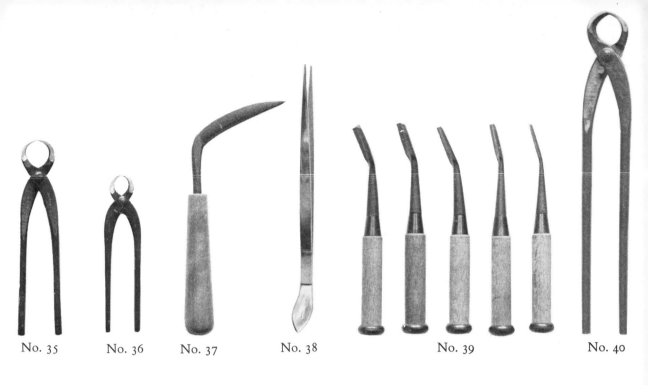

No. 35     No. 36     No. 37     No. 38     No. 39     No. 40

No. 101     No. 102     No. 116     No. 126     No. 128

No. 31 Nine-piece set
No. 32 Eight-piece set
No. 33 Five-piece set
No. 34 Three-piece set
No. 132 Seven-piece set
No. 35 Knot cutter, large
No. 36 Knot cutter, small
No. 37 Scythe for use in
     repotting
No. 38 Tweezers
No. 39 Chisels
No. 40 Root cutters for

Azaleas
No. 101 Handmade
     trimming shears
No. 102 Handmade
     trimming shears
     with long handle
No. 116 Nippers for twigs,
     small
No. 126 Lever, miniature
No. 128 Handmade
     trimming shears,
     medium

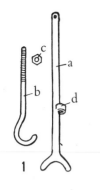

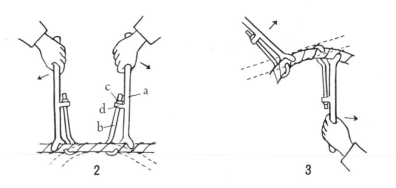

1    2    3

## Using the Lever

The lever can be of great use in correcting shapes of limbs and trunks that are too hard and stiff to be bent or straightened by hand. For example, as chart 2 shows, when a branch will not bend, first wrap it with wire then, apply one or two levers. By tightening nut *a* it is possible to adjust the length of key *b*. When the levers are firmly in place one may easily bend the branch into the desired shape. To straighten a bent branch, it is possible to set the levers as in chart 1 and reverse the process. But sometimes, the bend of the material makes this placement inconvenient. In such cases, set the levers closer together. Put on the top of and one underneath the branch as in chart 3. Two levers set in one place double the strength, although for most bonsai purpose one in each setting is adequate. There are many other uses for these handy tools, as the reader will learn as he experiments with them himself. The levers come in large and small sizes.

## Using the Jack

Like the levers, the jacks too come in large and small sizes. The small one is for use on branches with diameters of about two and one-half inches the large one for branches about three and one-half inches in diameter. First, disassemble the jack as shown in chart 1. Rod 2 reinforces the frame and makes possible the movement of part 3. Although the nuts at the ends of rod 2 require only light pressure to turn, they must fit in the groove at 4. Oiling parts that come into contact before use makes for smoother operation. The jacks and the levers are designed to be used together in the correction of bonsai limbs and branches. chart 1 chart 2 chart 3.

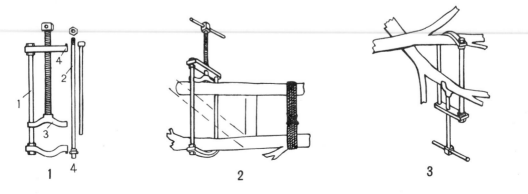

1    2    3

# 15. Bonsai Materials and How to Obtain Them (A Concise Chart)

| Plant | Repotting season | Watering | Fertilizing | Bud trimming and pruning | Wiring | Miscellaneous |
|---|---|---|---|---|---|---|
| **Black Pine** | Third to fourth year, early March to mid-May. | Likes sun. Water moderately. Water leaves from time to time in summer. | Place small amounts of oil cake on surface of soil in March, April, June, and October. | Trim green buds in April or May. Prune branches in March and September. Remove old leaves in September. | Between December and February or March of the following year. | If changing from a sandy to a less sandy soil, do so gradually. |
| **Red Pine** | Same as for black pine. | Same as for black pine. | Place small amounts of oil cake on surface of soil in March, June, and October. | Same as for black pine. | Same as for black pine. | The important point is to increase the number of small branches by trimming the green buds. |
| *Nishiki* **Pine** | Within a month of the vernal equinox of the second or third year. | Give plenty of sun and somewhat more water than for the black pine. | Fertilize as for the black pine but give young trees slightly more. | Trim green buds in April or May. Prune branches in September. Remove old leaves in September. | Between December and February or March of the following year. | Drainage must be very good; wet trunk before applying wire. |
| **Ezo Spruce** | Vernal equinox or September of the every second year for a young tree and of every fourth or fifth year for an old tree. | Water moderately but sometimes water the leaves. | About the same as for the five-needle pine.<br>— | Trim buds often between April and June. Prune branches in winter. | From November to about the end of February. | Keep well shaded after repotting; and be watchful for insects when new buds appear. |
| **Japanese Cedar** (*Cryptomeria*) | From March to May of the second year for a young tree and of the third year for older trees. | Water fairly frequently and well and wet the leaves from time to time. | Except for July and August, any time between the vernal equinox and October. At least once give fertilizer dissolved in water. | Trim buds in spring and fall; prune branches from February to mid-March. | In February or March. | Drainage must be very good; trim buds with fingertips only. |
| **Needle Juniper** | Between March and May of the third to fourth year. | The same as for the black pine. | Place small amounts of oil cake on the surface of the soil in April, June, and October. | Trim buds from time to time during period between spring and autumn; prune branches in early spring. | February to March. | Be careful of the low and medium branches which tend to wither easily. |

| Plant | Repotting season | Watering | Fertilizing | Bud trimming and pruning | Wiring | Miscellaneous |
|---|---|---|---|---|---|---|
| **Sargent Juniper** | From March till the end of May of every second year. | Water fairly plentifully and wet leaves often. | From the end of March till the beginning of June and then again from August to November alternate with placed oil cake and fertilizer dissolved in water. | Trim buds often from spring to autumn. Prune branches in early spring. | February to March. | Insects tend to plague these trees in March and April. |
| **Japanese Cypress** | From late March to mid-April every other year. | Water fairly often; it is almost never necessary to wet leaves. | Same as for juniper. | Trim buds two times between spring and summer and once in fall. Prune branches in autumn. | From February or March till mid-October. | Trim buds with fingertips only; do not expose to western sun. |
| **Maple** (*Momiji*) | At about the vernal equinox each year. | Once or twice a day in spring and autumn, two or three times a day in summer. | Three or four times a month from the time the buds appear until early June. Use a highly dilute fertilizer-water solution. | Trim buds when the new ones have begun to be active. Continue to trim from time to time as needed. Prune branches at repotting time. | Wire during the rainy early summer months. Use paper-wrapped wire. | Trim lateral buds quickly to make the branches and their ends fine and soft. |
| **Wax Tree** | Immediately after the buds appear every year. | Water as for most plants but avoid over-watering. | Once or twice a month from the time the buds become active until August. Use fertilizer dissolved in water. | When the new buds have grown out well, trim all but two or three leaves at the base in order to stimulate a second group of buds. | Wire old branches before the new buds appear; wire new branches in midsummer. | Avoid the western summer sun and store indoors in winter. |
| **Zelkova** | From the vernal equinox to mid-April every year. | Water well, wet the leaves from time to time, and protect from the western summer sun. | Using a very highly dilute fertilizer-solution, apply three or four times a month from the time the buds become active until midsummer. | Trim buds often from early spring and throughout the summer. Trim the most virgorous parts of the plant. | From June till July, but since the bark is tender use only paper-wrapped wire. | To protect the fine, tender small branches, store indoors in winter. |
| **Beech** | At about the vernal equinox every year. | Water once or twice daily in spring and autumn and two or three times daily in summer. It is unnecessary to wet leaves if the tree is kept where it comes in contact with evening dews. | Using fertilizer dissolved in water, apply twice monthly from the time the buds become active in spring until midsummer. | Leaving two or three leaves, trim the new buds as they appear. Prune branches at repotting time. | Mid- to late March and the rainy early summer period. | Since scale insects often attach themselves to these trees, wash the trunk in spring and summer. Keep well shaded in summer. |

| Plant | Repotting season | Watering | Fertilizing | Bud trimming and pruning | Wiring | Miscellaneous |
|---|---|---|---|---|---|---|
| **Oak** (*Quercus dentata*) | Just after the buds appear every year. | Water often enough to prevent drying out. In summer keep well shaded and protected from the western sun. | Using fertilizer-and-water solution, apply two or three times a month from the time the buds become active until midsummer. | Trim all but two or three leaves from new buds as they appear. Prune branches at repotting time. | June to mid-July. | Keep a watchful eye for ants who build their nests at the roots and for other insects that eat the leaves. |
| **Birch** | Yearly from the vernal equinox till early April. | Store in cool, shaded place in summer. Protect from western sun. Water well, and wet leaves often. | Using a dilute solution of water and the top clear liquid from an rotted mixture of oil cake, water, and a small amount of bone meal, fertilize two or three times before the beginning of the rainy early summer period. | Leaving two or three leaves at the base, trim new buds as they appear, until the beginning of early summer. | From early till mid-summer. | If the fertilizer contains too much nitrogen or if the air of the environment is dirty, the bark will not turn white. Water occasionally in winter. |
| **Maple** (*Kaede*) | Yearly from the time the buds become active until the vernal equinox. | Once or twice a day in spring and autumn and twice or three times a day in summer. In summer store in a cool shaded place out of the western sun. | The same as for maple (*momiji*). | Leaving two leaves at the base, trim new buds as they develop. Prune branches at repotting time. Prune leaves once or twice during the rainy early summer months. | In the early summer; always use paper-wrapped wire. | Store in a sunny place in spring and autumn. In pruning remove any branches that obstruct good lighting and ventilation. |
| **Plum** | Mid- to late March every year. Wait until flowers fall from trees in bloom. | Give the tree plenty of sunlight and water. From time to time in hot weather spray the leaves with a fine mist. | Using a dilute solution of animal fertilizer and water, apply once every ten days from May till June and four or five times from midsummer till September. | Trim old branches after the flowers fall and the new buds become active. When the new buds are well developed, trim their cores. Trim new branch buds as they appear. | In early June, instead of wiring, use a frame to correct the shape. | Keep a watchful eye for harmful insects. Never over water the blossoms. Protect plants repotted in autumn from winter frosts. |
| **Japanese Quince** | Either at the vernal equinox or from late September to mid-October yearly. | Keep in a sunny well ventilated place and water well. | Except for the rainy season and midsummer water fertilize twice a month as long as there are leaves on the plant; use a dilute solution of oil cake, bone meal, fish meal, and water. | Allow the new buds to grow long and thick. Remove only those that are not needed for the appearance of the tree. Prune the branches in late autumn, but be careful not to cut away excess buds. | Wire thick branches from June until mid-summer. Leave the wire in place for two or three years. | Remove buds when they seem excessively abundant. |

| Plant | Repotting season | Watering | Fertilizing | Bud trimming and pruning | Wiring | Miscellaneous |
|---|---|---|---|---|---|---|
| Peach | Yearly either around the vernal equinox or in October. | Water just enough to prevent excess wetness and dryness. | Using a water and fertilizer solution, apply in early spring and from the conclusion of flowering until October. | Cut branches short after flowering. Trim bud cores in June and prune branches from early spring until November. | June. | Peaches cannot stand severe cold. Keep them sheltered from frost in winter. |
| Cherry | The same as for peach. | Water with moderation. Store in a shaded place in summer. | It is easy to over-fertilize cherries. Use a dilute solution. Avoid animal fertilizers. Apply twice monthly until the end of September. | The same as for peach. | Using paper-wrapped wire, apply from late May till mid-June. | Do not tamper too much with the branches. Carefully remove insects and protect wounds in old trees from rotting. |
| Camellia | Late March for winter blooming trees; April or May from spring blooming plants. | Water as for most plants. Store in a shaded place in summer and protect from western sun. | Except for periods of extended rain or mid-summer, fertilize with a water-fertilizer solution twice a month from spring till fall. | Prune branches at repotting time and trim bud cores in June. | Wire with paper-covered wire in May or June. | Remove wire as soon as it has achieved its purpose. Protect from winter frosts. |
| Rose | Mid- to late June every year. | Water as for most plants and store in a well lighted well ventilated place. | From time to time fertilize with a very dilute solution of oil cake with bone meal or potassium sulphate. | Remove unwanted buds while they are small. Prune branches well back after blooming at repotting time. | Wire or train on a frame from June to July. | The stock plant will put out buds which must be trimmed away in early spring. |
| Cape Jasmine | Yearly at either the vernal or autumnal equinox. | Water with moderation. Keep in a sunny place. | Except for rainy periods and winter, fertilize with a dilute solution twice a month. | Trim the bud cores before early June; prune branches at repotting time. | May or June. | Shade well in summer. Bonsai may be raised from cuttings or by layering other cape jasmine plants. |
| Wisteria | Yearly at the vernal equinox or in June. | Keep in a sunny place and water well. In summer set container in a basin partly filled with water. | Using a dilute solution, fertilize weekly from the time the flowers fall until midsummer. | Prune branches after the flowrs fall, in June, in midsummer, and again in autumn. Leave the short branches uncut. | Using paper-wrapped wire, train after the flowers on new branches fall. | Do not cut the thick roots. Do not allow to dry out either in summer or winter. |
| Rhododendron | Every second year in either mid- or late October or April. | Water well and expose to night dews. In summer keep in a cool shaded place. | Fertilize once monthly till september with a dilute solution made from a rotted mixture of oil cake and bone meal with water. | Prune branches at repotting time. Trim buds before June and from time to time as required. | Using paper-wrapped wire, apply fairly tightly in mid-June. | Drainage in the pot must be good. Water moderately in summer. |